Thank you for
Your Support!
Bob !!

Big Hugs!

The Paradigm

Poetry Through Life's Lessons

by Lashea M. Johnson

authorHOUSE®

AuthorHouse™
1663 Liberty Drive
Bloomington, IN 47403
www.authorhouse.com
Phone: 1-800-839-8640

First published by AuthorHouse 4/1/2010

ISBN: 978-1-4490-9864-3 (e)
ISBN: 978-1-4490-9863-6 (sc)

Library of Congress Control Number: 2010904140

Printed in the United States of America
Bloomington, Indiana

This book is printed on acid-free paper.

Photography by Ernestine Willis-Adams

Dedication

To my children: Darius, Lauren, Whitney and Angela...

There is nothing that can suffice the time wasted between us; there is only the time that we hold now to make the difference. I pray for your healing from the wounds that I have caused. I acknowledge my mistakes and my shortcomings and I apologize, with the promise of recovery for as long as eternity can rent to me to grant to you.

I love you with all that I am,

Mom

Introduction

During the process of life there are words and expressions used to sum up a situation or an event that has taken place in or around our lives.

You are about to embark on some spoken word entries that have gotten me   through some tough times I'm talking hair pulling on your knees graveling praying to God crying, what in the ham-sandwich is going on asking, singing how did I get here!

We all go through things in life and sometimes we think that we are alone. I am that voice that shares with you, the true fact that you are not alone.

As my mother use to say, "There is nothing new under the sun." Need I tell you? She is right.

We can get ourselves into some pretty interesting situations...soul searching ones, regretful dangerous and sometimes fatal ones. Many times we have prayed that prayer, "God if you just get me out of this one I'll do better, be better and before you can bat your eyes you're right back in another fox-hole praying.

Some of us make it, we change. Other's are still struggling or have perished along the way inside or outside of their mess. In reading me I know that you will hear or see yourself, a family member or close friend because truly we are all connected and affected in one form or another. Life is busy, I heard somewhere that "knowledge is power" I beg to differ, I believe that: **"applied knowledge is power."**

I have to do this I have to share screaming at the top of my lungs I will, in order to prevent or shorten the length and reason for loss. ...The loss of time, negative energy and unnecessary struggles. If you were standing in the middle of the street and a truck was coming wouldn't you want for me to warn you?

Right?!

This is what this is all about…loss prevention, I'm doing security and I can not allow loss on my watch. Our living through lesson's and experience can not be in vain. Pride…guilt and shame can not be the obstacles that stop us from helping.

Every form of instances in life we go through are in order to help others, to be a blessing an informant, this is my way of embracing you. Over the pages filled with ink and truth I am a voice an informant, in a descriptive language of experience and circumstance.

I am sharing these episodes and thoughts out of care, concern and love. I hope that my pieces enlighten and inspire as well as help you. Make you think and allow you to see that we are not unique in this world of trials, tribulations, persecutions, thoughts, fears and dreams, or in search of answers.

You are not alone.

And…We are not perfect but we can strive to become on a daily basis. God judging us in the end is what we should consider. For me this journey has been a turbulent, in and out of valley traveling, self check seeking, starting with the man in the mirror facing- learning experience. I had to come to terms with accepting and finding the will to want a positive transition. (CHANGE)

It is my destiny and yours to be an inspiration; Open up your eyes, take a seat and turn your mind on! For sure it will not be left empty…

Sincerely,

La'Shea M. Johnson

The Table of Contents

The Basement...

From the corner to the hallways or abandoned buildings to the basement as to jails, Institutions and eventually Death...

Like most addicts there are dealers that eventually become addicts themselves or die before going to jail.

Like prostitutes as to pimps from the corner to the block strips, laid out in territorial maps by the so called callers...ballers as so named.

Runaways, castaways, drifters and loners; Regular people that have given up on life so now they are controlled. Ran down, ran up and down to the sort of nothingness that stresses the so called normal eye.

Like policemen, vice and the D.E.A all the way to the F.B.I Corrupt and as crooked as a five year old coloring out side of the lines struggling to get it straight. From raids to planting drugs and surveillance cameras out on a stake out...and snitches and set ups in frames wide enough to hang us all.

From the tables and chairs that seat addicts neatly in a circle to snort, smoke, shoot up while exchanging stories of who they use to be, as to what they have or had back when, promising that one day they are going to stop using people and themselves.

Short or long stories of how they ended up in the basement in the first damn place.

Stories about who died and why...

Stories about who went through the pockets and stole form the dead before calling the police.

Tales about how Nea- Nea died and they dumped her body in the alley... arguments of shorting the split, running off with the cut and paybacks.

Tales of Beth carrying her baby but can't stop smoking while in labor and moving the plate closer for one more hit off her crack pipe. as her water breaks and blood runs down her legs, with on lookers shaking their heads as they continued to snort, smoke or shoot up. While some concerned addict rushes her out basically to steal what she has left as they close and lock the door behind her…

Tales of Lori Wahl, she OD off of anti-depressants and street drugs of how they moved her body from the table to the hallway…as cameras and lights peered on and word spread all across the 5 0'clock news.

From the suburbs, to the corners, to the hallways and abandoned buildings, to...
...The Basement.

Addicted….

Blowing out smoke
picking at this tugging at that
looking around out the window between this and that
under this and that on the floor still in search for just one more...

...Coming up with schemes wasting time
Robberies hold ups, bad checks in lines
Returns hell donate blood
food stamps, wic coupons
gift certificates nothing was to
Intricate…

Mob action give a ways,
run a ways,
fools carrying around paraphernalia tools,
squats here and there closed or out in the open...

Got to get that ill off no matter how,
 Where or when, but now
up my nose in my vein
smoke in my mouth straight through to my brain.

Tweak this and tweak that
got to hurry and get back,
take this hit to the head the arm the
nose…
glasses tinted with rose,
no more pain
no feelings at all…
blowing out smoke.

Smelling bad no soap or water,
selling everything you had and your self cheap
…and no food to eat.
In the stores stealing meat,

maybe chips here or there,
or just a cigarette…
Too much despair.

Hair undone looking unnatural, the walking dead passed by a mirror and still you said," not bad, looking good." Meanwhile you're just a bone who's souls about to be hauled home in a bag or box with a whole lot of chatter, get it together! …See the matter?

I know… I'm just blowing out smoke.
By LMJ

Department Of Corrections, (D.O.C)...

Take your clothes off! Medical history has to
be done! Blood drawn, pap smear.
Squat, cough, raise your nipples, spread your ass
cheeks, wave your fingers through your hair.
Open your mouth and lift your tongue.

Do you know where you are...D.O.C?

Blue suits worn a thousand times before and after you by any one it
would fit or NOT.

Thick sliced bologna so thick that it can't be flushed down
the toilet, two slices of wet or dry bread maybe
W/mustard or with out, If you're lucky a juice and
or a piece of fruit, a bag of chips…hum
...If no one has stolen it first,

The sound of your cell-e regurgitating up their
insides of the blows inside or NOT,
Constant flushing that rings through out the
entire jail from one end to the other.

Whispers heard in the dark at night once each door is locked through
the vents. Who are you what's your name? You sound good, sing
somebody (as someone sings in the back ground), that *****! Hook me
up, I got you boo; go on through the night and until those who aren't
crying for their first time on the inside or dope sick fall finally off to
sleep.

Do you know where you are...D.O.C?

Standing at the locked door agitated waiting for the sound of the
clicking and the popping of the doors set off round and round, to
laugh, watch TV, talk about God and read your bible, or your case.
Argue, eat,

Sneak hugs and kisses and maybe more depending on who you are. Until the resounding sounds of the clicking and the popping of the doors note;

Take it in for shift change and head count until lunch or dinner time!

Do you know where you are ...D.O.C?

Opposition dressed up and down in darker blues and spit shinned shoes, the jingling of keys and heavy hefty voices filled with all of that authority. Hated, be-friended, favored or NOT... mm the turn key. For those cast aside from their families to work below minimum wages for a piece of independence and a slice of freedom in its own way of out side of the cell privileges.

Cliques: pretty, money, ugly, power: translated
as juice, poor commissary whore.
Begged borrowed friends, stole, hustled, permed,
curled and even dyed hair, crop cuts...
Ironed pressed mattress suits, worn in pride or NOT...

Until that day comes that's long for by some or NOT...
Pack It UP!! Hey D.O.C, you...26th street bus waiting,
phone call making, cold Pepsi drinking, fried chicken
eating, filtered cigarette smoking, civilian clothes wearing
take it in when you get ready to self trying to
Have somebody to come pick you up...girl, boy,
so where are you now? Free or NOT...

By LMJ

...While You Were Away...

While you were away getting high all of the
wonders of life passed you by...
Your children grew up without you and don't
even have a clue as to, who they are.

Time passed by and change happened while you got high and mind
sucked into an oblivion unfamiliar to those around you,

While you were away getting high, the seasons changed, hell the shows
on TV changed, the president changed bills and rights and laws in
congress changed, the Skyline down town Chicago changed the design
on dollar bills and coins changed...

Presidents changed, the shape of your body changed, all the while you
were stuck and dope fiend mind sucked into believing and receiving
the short ends of stickups jail time and baggies, needles and straws,
mirrors and razors and crack head tours...

Fashions changed, hair styles changed, mathematical systems changed,
the value of life for you had some how changed into something less
then zero.

While you remained basically: pathetically, unconsciously, unaware,
unmoved of being stressfully, hurtfully and sadly...the same...

Without Change... things stay the same ...

To change is to grow with purpose and meaning in life and love while
sharing and giving of yourself...

Others have missed you including me...

Won't you come back to the place you should be... to live to love and
fulfill your destiny It's not too late...

By LMJ

Addicted Men Folk...

I am so lame. I don't have enough confidence to approach a woman, solely based on who I am and truthfully with out a gimmick. So I buy drugs and I make my presence known to them. I be-little them, I degrade them all for the need of self gratification and power.

I string them along and cheat them, I use them until I'm tired or something fresh comes along or I run out of money, which ever comes first or first to last, because they don't know. I am a liar, a thief and a murderer killing that which is good and created by God, both of our souls...

Hell! I figure they don't mind they go for it because truly they don't want me, they just want what I have. This hurts so I inflict more pain by shortening the gimmick. Teasing them making them do what ever I please bend over backwards or down on their knees, because I just want to see how far they are willing to go.

Some follow suit, some walk away (merely a yet for them too) but for those who stay they are my rappies, my partners in crime. Forgetting that I have created soul ties, they are used as my muse in my addiction all the while I blot out all that I am doing wrong.

They...

They have a choice. But the gimmick calls to them and to me and I keep going until nothing is left.

Then of course they leave me alone and feeling as stupid is as stupid does, to think about how I'm going to do things differently the next time. Not even remembering that what goes around comes around and worse...

The gimmick is gone and all that is left is... I wish ...I wish...I wish.

By LMJ

Another Brother Gone…

Street crimes, games, gangs and drugs neighborhood thugs…

Heroin, marijuana, crack cocaine only the players have changed, the rest remains the same. Dope dealers, prostitutes gambling casting lots futuristic money won for their own burial plots.

Gunshots fired! Sirens ring out loud another innocent killed in the crowd another is dead…m-m it's another brother just another brother is gone. Hymns and preachers flowers and food receptions of families in altered moods, music… dance grievances weighed but can't be denied. Mother, sister, father and the tears they cry.

Another brother is gone and to this we have gotten use, a new dealer now holds the juice. Long black cars, in rows and lines, smelling the scent of fresh cut pine… awaiting the next to drop the dime.

Beneath the ground and through the air heart ache travels in despair for the pain of the reign of another brother gone. Cremated, ashes to ashes dust to dust rested silently in a vase adorned upon the mantle piece or scattered across the sea another brother is gone could've been you, could've been me… so its not just…

Another Brother gone.

By LMJ

In Between...

Decisions,   Decisions,   Decisions!

This or that, he or she, him or her, mother or father, sister or brother, man or woman lover.

Live or die, obey or disobey, stay or run away, light or dark, do or don't, can or won't, tell the truth or tell a lie, move forward or go backward, sideways, left or right, bring or leave behind, to keep or throw away to love or to hate.

Decisions,   Decisions,   Decisions!

Heaven or hell, hot or cold, young or old, tender or tough, easy or hard, stop or start to give in or give up, get up or lay down, to wear a smile or a frown to be or not to be...

Give me a hint give me a clue what am I suppose to do?

Decisions,   Decisions,   Decisions!

First follow then lead, listen to be heard, understand to be understood, do something or do nothing when you know not what to do.

I gave you a hint I gave you a clue so now it's up to you.

Decisions,   Decisions,   Decisions!

In between or betwixt put you life in the mix, get up when you fall down, wear a smile not a frown, you'll laugh and you'll cry all of this is a part of life.

You then me, he then she, us then we, to live or to die, to be or not to be...

Decisions,   Decisions,   Decisions!

By LMJ

The Looking Glass...

There I was just standing, talking and congregating with my sisters and savoring the taste of freedom.

Joy and peace all rapped up in a white paper
bag filled with sweet, sweet cookies.
Oatmeal raisin, butter and sugar ones. Looking
and pointing outward at the looking glass.

You then Me, us then we... Seeing the beast the ghost,
The host inside of the pain, In the last ride of the white stallion,
The Rough Rider harshly showed up inside
her and out into the looking glass...

The slow blow of smoke, the silent jokes told by passersby and deep down inside my soul I cried of memories not long past from this look I got, looking into the looking glass...

Like plums to raisins, raisins in the sun dried up and undone, unnatural made into a spectacle underneath a microscope...

Standing, walking and running miserably sideways for one more bag of hope lost inside a bag of dope...

..All of this I seen sight and words unspoken on this mystery I was choking, coughing up thanks joy and tears putting behind me all of my fears that I'd seen briefly, summing up what use to be me... use to be me... use to be me...

..On the other side of the looking glass.

By LMJ

An Illusion...   For Mattie;

Decisions demonic elements spirits of past lives haunts and taunts being chased by some entity invading my space; I saw them they were there people screaming there's nothing to fear but I saw them I know I did.

Some happy most angry why is this happening to me? If I can just stay awake I'll make it through the night, my soul is tired but still I fight. Swish...swishing my towels in the air swinging at what isn't there, I saw them I know I did.

So they say I'm insane I'm crazy there are screws loose just because you can't see them you judge me harshly but they are there. I fight, I talk back to them yes they do hear me listen and understand me clearly...

You say my mind is gone I know when I swish my towels in the air at the spirits I know are there, is this my destiny that I project from some unnatural thing that I suspect has had his hand and eye on me for something before that I could not see?

Will I come back to the world where you live? is there no peace, no peace for me or will my damnation elude me for the son who died for me, now his face I shall not see... but the spirits, decisions, demonic elements of past lives now my haunts on them I thrive, swishing my towels through the air, one shot one pill, I'm in despair but no one knows.

I wash the walls with my bible, I talk to them as they talk to me I see them as plain as you see me, I saw them I know I did. Grabbing, snatching staking a claim for my life my husband cheated on me his wife, dressed down and up, smoke like phantoms in the air I see them every where, not goblins and ghouls from trick or treat these spirits they talk to me, I saw them I know I did.

I long to rest to sleep in peace but there's no where to rest my weary feet, I walk the floors all night long hoping soon to be carried home no rest for them no rest for me while you're snuggled between your sheet.

They are every where be it light or dark they just don't care I can see them and they see me this is my reality.

So go ahead heed the call less you be over taken by a fall and then you'll see…

Decisions, demonic elements spirits of past lives up in hell you'll lift up your eyes unless you get down on your knees pray cry out, cry out for help, peace and joy praise the lord and shout forever more no more no more illusions to explore lift up your hands put down I my towels for this will be my sacred vow,

>   …But I saw them I know I did.
>   BY LMJ

He Loved Me First...

I turned my back on the man that loves me the most.

He tells me all that I or any other woman would like to hear...
If and when I am hungry, he provides. Out of all the time that I've been on this earth he has ensured me that he would always be there for me.

He is a comforter,
A great companion, he is strong and beautiful and sensitive to my needs and sometimes I don't even have to tell him what's wrong with me, he just knows.
I miss him.

If I could find this man again truly in my
heart I would never let him go again.
I know that he is not far away; if I call him... will he answer?

I've ran from him back and forth not knowing what it was that I really had and now... I'd like to find out. I want to know him, to trust him, to love him as he has loved me.

He is a teacher a man that makes you look at his responses in wonder... an excellent lover, loves me the way no other has or ever could.

I felt him once or twice way down deep in my soul and the feeling;
...indescribable, but a joy.

...Easy to talk to. Even when I don't know how or what to say to him, he understands and encourages me to come closer to him in a bond strong enough," he said" to make us perfect and whole, one with each other.

I miss him.

Sometimes I don't understand why he does some of the things he does, or says and sometimes I even have the nerve to question him, when I know that he has my best interest a heart.

He is a creator, Oh! you should see some of the things he has made... sunshine, moonshine, hot and cold in weather, branched pieces of wood with pretty green leaves colorful to the eyes.

Ideas and bone structure and red juices on which and why I live!

Oh! I could go on and on about him and one day I will, but right now. I just really need to find him...
I miss him.

By LMJ

Know Better...

Old Folks saying goes "When you know better do better."

Chile yo mama didn't raise you up like this, you know better. Shift she'd turn and twist knowing you out doing stuff like this...

Spending all of her time in church heeding alter call, breast feeding, breakfast making, lunch hauling, dinner calling you down stairs to feed yo sorry but...

Chile yo mama didn't raise you up like this, do better. Sent you to school to learn, all of her days of hard work for she yearned for you to have, to make something of yourself.

...Old folks saying goes," when you know better do better!"

By LMJ

Run Slave Run…

Master got you swinging high and low from his glass branches…
Master got you picking white balls off of
the floor and off of the wool on
Somebody else's back…

Master got you for his bed warmer, passes you around and sells you
cheap.

Master got you walking around ducking
supposed white sheets and stuck
In paranoia.

Master refuses to let you have your freedom…you so tired, so weak to
even fight back…

So…you wait, you swing from his glass
branches high and low, well I'm
Going to tell you what you need to know…

Master ain't got any real power over you; he only does what you let
him do.

Listen to me let me make it clear; it's his job to instill fear, he'll make
you feel alone and ostracized too…telling you, "get down slave do what
you got to do."

Take away things that are important and good for you…
Laugh and joke in your face while nothing is funny and you'll laugh
too, that's just how stuck Master's got you…

…But I tell you now…Run, Run, Run slave, Run!

By LMJ

Your Mind...

Dominating and strong filled with the promise of all things to come and things that have been published before you and interpreted by you in your own way...

The way that you think as power travels as an instinct seeking...
Hunting and endeavoring to bring into existence the nature of all that has happened to you, with you and around you, your evolvement...

Your Mind...

Like many others contemplating the where,
when, who, how and why of things...
Solutions, equations systematically adding, dividing
and subtracting the sum of things...

Reading and deciding, planning and providing
a list of things to go over to do,
To live and become...to surrender to...

Beautiful in essence of art of rhythm and rhyme intriguing me time after time after time and again...

I lose myself comfortably, hopelessly, and immensely you captivate me with,

...Your mind.

By LMJ

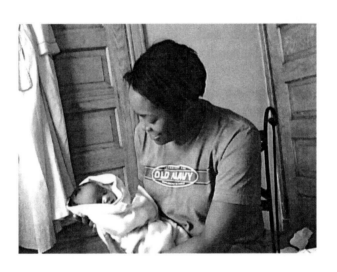

My Baby...

Change the baby, feed the baby, take the baby to the doctor, and wake up with the baby, wash the baby, clothe the baby, comb the baby's' hair, give medication to the baby, put the baby to sleep, play, sing, teach, love the baby...

Alone.

Then you wonder, you throw a tantrum with all of that hum drum, when I ask you or tell you what she needs, you're all mouth with a few simple deeds of what you should be doing...In the first place.

Telling me that our baby stuff,
I've had enough and enough is enough!

She is my baby...yeah sure with your DNA, yeah you through a few bumps and grinds well don't forget mines, I threw a pelvis move or two well what was I suppose to do? Surely I couldn't leave it all up to you.

...Some things you just can't do...ALONE,

I know I know it's the same old song. Song by millions of women that lost a burden Oh, my bad, a man that just wasn't willing to step up to the plate after he ejaculated...

Telling me that our baby stuff...
No family time, just things, things that are far and few and in between.

Let's be real, go ahead say it! Don't worry, I will...

She is my baby...and I don't mean mama's maybe!

By LMJ

No Puppet Here...

This string and that connected to each limb in space in my mind?

No, no puppet here...

Do this, do that, wear this or that, no thinking
of my own, no thoughts or ideas
Only broken speech impairments of what you
want to be, my down sized mind
That you've decided to trample on...

No, no puppet here...

Sex on command by your demand, you willing
away my dreams, my feelings and
Emotions and all I receive is a token of what
you deem to be pleasurable for me?

No, no puppet here...

How confused you must be to think that I'd allow you to trifle over
me.

Misused and abused, no I'm not confused breaking down and trifling
over my self esteem, clip snipping my butterfly wings, you predicate
endless words and empty... they are.

Hello Barney, hello dumb- dumb.

No... baby WRONG girl there are... No puppets here.

By LMJ

Love Me...

I like the way you say my name, love me...

Tell me that I'm beautiful, that's right love me...

Kiss me behind my neck and my ears m-m your kisses feel so good right there, love me...

Cuddle me; cradle me in your arms m-m your body feels so nice and warm, that's right, love me...

Stand by my side, but tell when I'm wrong, m-m
touch me your touch is so right, so strong
that's right love me...

I'll tell you my secrets you tell me your needs,
Sweet Mountain dew honey bee's m-m-m
baby that's right love me...

I'll clutch your head between my breast on my stomach rest your chest
m-m love me...

Dreams had loves fill souls and bodies joined
God's will. Matrimony joyful wedded bliss
m-m I never thought I could feel like this, m-m m-m love me...

Both of our love stands tall and strong we're where
God intended, where we both belong
m-m touch me, love me, hold me, kiss me...

I want to be with you for the rest of my life, you
my husband and I your wife, kiss me..
..that's right kiss me m-m, m-m, m-m love me.

By LMJ

Deep down inside…

There is a yearning a burning a sensation reaching seeping calling out for so many things all of which they say God brings, in his time they also say. What, I say? When I 'm in pain or feeling lost and deprived of love happiness and joy, the kind that you see with kids and their brand new toy, how they scream and shout jumping all about on the out side or within, large smiles and foolish grins…

Some say that, that kind of love only exist in fantasies well I'll take the fantasy world of that particular portion. I see love and other people happy every time I listen to music or read even when I watch TV, what of my love what about me?

NO, not the simulations thereof but the real deal, not an obsession or infatuation, one of protection and understanding and observation of one's nature and intuitive sublime realization of each touch each stroke of the hand or tongue of all that is pure and natural, for me to me, with me and in me. There it is that yearning and burning again that sensation reaching seeping calling out for so many things, all of which God brings, in his time.

Positively and surely my time is coming though it is not here I'll just yearn and burn with these sensations that seep and call out for so many things all of which God brings in his time…but I wish so deeply that the time was in fact now.

Ordained am I to wait for my destiny my fate? For the happiness and joy that of a kid with a brand new toy, for this time in which he shall quench the yearning and burning of this sensation reaching seeping calling out for so many things all of which God brings in his time, one of protection and understanding and observation of one's nature and intuitive sublime realization of each touch, each stroke of the hand or tongue of all that is pure and natural, for me, to me, with me and in me… I know my time will come but in his time.

By LMJ

My Beacon...

Dark and lonely nights with tears in my eyes, pain and aches in my heart and soft muffled cries...

When I didn't know where to go or who to turn to, or how to start my life anew...just one look at you...

Bottles made, your diaper changed and your appointments are all arranged, the songs I've sang while looking into your eyes, the very beating of your heart...

Your smiles and sleepy grins right down to the dimple in your chin...
Holding your hands, playing with your toes,
you're sweet and perfect God knows...
Combing your hair, watching you grow daily,
Washing and dressing you in your pretty little clothes...

Wondering to myself, who am I raising? to be in
this world my fine wild eye baby girl...
Lord, who will she be? What is her destiny? ...praying to be able
to do the best that I can in one of my parts in Gods' great plan...

You are my beacon an extreme bright light sent to me by God to end my dark and lonely nights, my hope in a world that's beaten and torn...

The possibilities changed the moment you were born...
...especially for me,

A pure dream in a world so impure your innocence is the ultimate allure and cure of the future...

It is from you that I aspire to be, in Gods' will what is meant for me,

Erin... you are my beacon, an extreme bright light...

I Love you...all my Love, Mommy.

By LMJ

Dreams...

Soft melodies of joy and hope for the future that
float through our subconscious minds...
Visions of what we could possibly be at our best...

Sweet and never ending extensions of what we wish for in this life
time...

Branded so deeply within us that they invade us as we sleep, talk and
breathe...

Bringing them into existence by word of mouth and the sweat of our
brows' they come true and there we are wishing and hoping once
again...

With the same joy and sense of a dream to accomplish what it really
means to fulfill anything...

...With a heightened sense of enthusiasm because now we believe.

Warm and cuddle-ly fuzzy and slippery pink and purple elements
peering out at us blinking into reality rays of sunshine, yellow and
bright, warm and wanting...

In meeting them we meet ourselves face to face...

...Before we choose them openly and hopefully with approval from
none here on earth.

Dreams...Can't live with out them.

You So Crazy...

Mm, must have slipped your mind talking and singing, mixing rhymes... talking of things in and out of sense, pretense. as intense as it sounds its really not.

You So Crazy...

Mm, thinking and dreaming of how you could possibly have a better life some day. Adding and multiplying your dreams times a higher power... talk of how and what he can do.

Reading and obtaining knowledge so that your family will have a better chance at life, you show do a lot of thinking and organizing and planning and dreaming and hoping.

You say you pray and your knowledge comes from there, Mm..

You So Crazy...

Mm, when they spoke of Martin and Malcolm and Nelson and even ol' Abe of having insight and wishing the people well...that one day their children would have stories to tell..

About,

A Revolution..
Slavery..
Segregation..
The Apartheid..
and Independence..

Singing spirituals, protest, long walks and papers being signed.
Some even doing jail time.
I tell you people always got something negative to say, you know what they said before any of these things actually happened?

...You So Crazy!

By LMJ

About A Woman...

Bra's, panties, slips, lips, hips, finger-tips, toes control top pantyhose, perfumed earlobes, neck breast and thighs. Sparkling twinkles in their eyes.

Sway back dresses and chiffon blouses,
candles and flowers in their houses
Ivory snow white teeth, shimmering subtle
soft skin beneath the sheets.

Gliding to music without a care a sweet aroma left in the air...

Recipes from days of old taught not to give away the gold...

Dreams of families and friends dinner on the town or midnight dances with gentlemen callers sitting fire side in the courting parlor...

Swept away by day or by night, any woman's fantasy delight...

Cherries, chocolate éclairs, lemon moraine pies
walk on the beach toe to toe eye to eye
My love was dancing with the moon I'll be there; I'll be home soon...

What a man loves most about a woman, she is his close friend, his partner and lover.

Re-living memories of a sister a mother,
loving his wife and his daughter...
...least any man should boast of...

What a man loves most- About A woman.
By LMJ

Your Passion...

You got to get up off of your inhibitions and stop wishing and do something   with that talent that God gave you...

... Yet you're stagnating wasting time the pace at which you could face your greatest triumphs, over obstacles and small road blocked bumps-yeah, I know that we are all bucking to get over the hump...

...So we try. We dust ourselves off and try again and again until we get it right.

You got to get up and face the situation, address it like a
stamp on an envelope and transfer it through the postal
station, like the president addresses the nation,
...Like God does upon every one of his creations.

You got to get up and make it happen...
Share your God given talent...
What would your life be like without passion...

...and you're not dead yet so ...

GET UP!

By LMJ

Use Protection…

…Not just from STD infections or as a birth control tool, but to prevent your self from appearing the fool, exploited and used tossed aside and emotionally drained and confused.

I know that your parents told it to you… you know just wait.

Wedding rings and upscale cakes toasting
high with champagne glasses…
Tuxedo and wedding gown dances…
Honeymoon getaways and staring glances…
A life time of possibilities and unbridled romancing…

Don't be no fool… and this is coming from old school.. to you, use protection.

…and for the rest of your life you'll share in an intimate affection taught in love and of a guided direction made by an observation of ones nation handed down throughout the generations… in love.

…Simply, use protection.

By LMJ

Call Me Crazy…

Call me crazy but I want;

Crazy ridicules I can't live with out you
consuming way down deep fire burning
Inside love churning turning…

Butterfly jittering, finger licking, lip smacking,
toe tapping, and cuddle napping,
Star gazing,

A wonderfully amazing hand holding, smile cajoling, public kissing,
starlight wishing…

Popcorn movie watching…sweetheart baby,
honey calling darling talking,
Beach walking, together we can make it kind of love.

So… If you can't provide these things then STOP wasting my time!

By LMJ

America….

Creepy Seepy thoughts decimation, consecration, aggravation, dissimilation of all human relations.

Needy feedy mouths consumption, salvation, aviation, starvation contemplation of every nation as to where and when the end comes after the moon or before the sun
America…?

Degradation humiliation voices in salutation, congregating and emancipating of the jaws gyrating, the invigorating savoring the taste that's consummating our bodies and life's blood.

Greedy Government vows to change things re-
arrange things, bringing things of all
Proportions together…
Lying, testifying, genociding, cultivating and administrating,
stealing and wheeling-dealing Nations…

Lost and gone wrong. So what of the National
Anthem, the Nations' song?
Land of the free?
Home of the brave?
More like the rich get richer and the poor remain slaves!

Scary hairy bugs… West Nile filled bugs,
neighborhoods that sell non-prescription drugs.
Bombs bursting in air and families in despair.

No movement,
No movement of bugs government sprayed
pesticides gave us soapsuds in tide,
What of the pilgrims' pride?

> The ramparts we watched?
> The ramparts we watched?

From the cradle to the grave: Jesus died that we might be saved. Not enslaved, over worked and under paid or even made...

John the Baptist did wade prayed and in the water he stayed, for the Consecration of All Nations through Christ that we may have life and that more abundantly.

Call it! Call it redundant that we transformed
it and made it what we wanted.
On the front and back of Bills slated and stated "In God We Trust."
But the Nations are heated and hated.
...Upon this rock on which we stand...No...
Not above board but on sinking sand.

America? Wake Up!!!

By LMJ

You Need To Stop Reading...

Information transferred into knowledge inspired by power recognized to the reader was scary.

Young blooded blacks hid to learn. Beat and burned, hung and hog tied most of whom have even died.

You Need To Stop Reading...

Slavery labeled drugs as power in dead presidents through out hints of the fast money made by the young black slave standing on the corner hustling.

...Traffic. Busy-busy, rocks, blows med-line.
As a sign hung in the balance, "Black Man Endangered Species," rested side ways off the wall.

You Need To Stop Reading...

Sign the dotted line by the X_____ and you have the right to remain or stay dead or even silent, the right to live and be loud or a slave in a crowd of many, that don't read but are shipped, slaughtered, sold or told and has excepted what was said.

You Need To Stop Reading...

To loose your land, your legacy, your birthright, your freedom, your life, your loved ones, your dignity your power to remain as dumb found slaves under the power of all dead presidents.

Inspired by staff person: Lou

By LMJ

See What I See…

Turned to us and said; I want to apologize to
my family and to my children with a
Straight but slightly crocked face…

I saw hurt, I saw fear, I saw expectation, I saw
courage and something imitating
Strength,

I saw year passing by and age and perhaps
wisdom seeping slowly in along with
Reality,

I saw a smile, I saw years before now back
when we were children and he saved
Me from the elements of the neighborhood and there I
stood then I sat and all that I could do was cry.

For a brief crumbling moment I could imagine
my ancestors watching idly by as
Their children were sold, whipped and tore away from them,(
I could relate) dared to see the future of my brothers' fate.

I saw a man growing not knowing his purpose
but on a journey to find out just what
Little boys are made of.

My heart ached for his children, for my mother
and I prayed that her heart would be
Strong enough to withstand the blow as it had
so many times before stood and stand
She did…

As she spoke of her only son and longing to spend some of her years
with him on this here earth. My heart shrank and everything inside of
me bellowed for God to fix this and to give us strength.

That which was last will one day be first, do
Gods' will and let nature take its' course,
…joy, pain, longsuffering, peace and love…see what I see

…I love you Aaron.

By LMJ

Mind over Matter...

Never mind the walls or the people with in them. The sounds, the silence, the ignorance, the pain, the love, the despair, the staff, the ones in charge.

The janitors, the social workers, the fast food workers, the long lines, the short tempers, the hot and cold days and nights, the love flow, the boxing blow.

Voices of yesterday the sounds of pitter patter its all mind over matter. The depression and salvation the use of drugs for self medication, the families with real big hugs, and back stabbers in your path lets not forget the aftermath.

Pills, shots, prescribed medications the doctor's and nurses at the nursing station. Shared tools, is education. Searching for direction and affection, and protection striving to avoid dereliction and degradation... questions in hesitation the end? No. you're your own Foe or maybe a friend. A prune, raisins, grapes, plumes in or out of season or any old shrub bed reason, we must find answers that are not of treason to ourselves...

Mind over matter mood altering drugs, cleaning, dusting old antique rugs, clothes stained of another's blood, trauma in the neighborhoods. ...And who cares?

Teachers, pastors, doctors and leaders yeah they intrigue us. Straight jackets, shots and pills, government ran ideals then filing court processed appeals...getting rich from what you've learned, but if its not right then you'll burn.. burn.. burn...

Mind over matter; Pain, pleasure, love, hate, destiny, fate, hunger, anger, the lonely, the young, the old and the terrified...

Mind over Matter?

By LMJ

Men Do Leave...

-Yeah they do, after they've planted their seed.
Yeah after the I love you and the golden rules that they, themselves
partake in egging you on to break, as they kiss you on the cheek then
neck and succeed in making your panties wet.

Exclaiming that they need time to think about
things...yeah like the next piece of ass
They're going to hit, lick and stick and then split.

Screaming profanities about how they got "baby mama
drama" in this state and that one. trying to get a nut, be it
Between her legs in her mouth or her but,

+
Grandma Always said, a stiff dick ain't got no conscience!

-Yeah they leave with our trust, our hopes and our dreams, for some
broken families... and what about the children?

They're still trying to pass the buck; hell na'll the buck stops here!

They aint stuck except on that weak ass excuse, exclaiming that they
need time to think about things.

Men do leave...weak men and good riddance!

By LMJ

Mm- Mm- Mm food...

Burgers, fries, shakes, chicken wings and
things, food makes my heart sing.
My toes curl and my heart skips a beat,
every time I pass by McDonalds I
Squirm in my seat.

Burger King broiled by my style you should the smile on my face child,
the Whopper w/cheese just can't be beat, I stuff myself so, I fell off my
feet can't tie my shoes or even see my stomach.

All because I can't pass up a line and in the drive thru all of the time,
Ordering...2 all beef patties special sauce,
lettuce, cheese on a sesame seed bun.
...Got to get me some of that um num num.

I'm not anorexic or maybe obesity is my fate? Hey wait, wait Popeye's
Chicken hot barbeque wings, blue cheese dressing is this a dream?
Hot diggidy dog Pizza King ya'll Home Run in now you're talking,
Churches Chicken all stop squawking.

Greasy crusted chicken, buttermilk biscuits the more I talk the longer
my list gets!

Alice's Barbeque, J&J Fish food would be my only wish
it makes me happy and fills my taste buds with harmony
but I'm so big no one or no one can lift me...
Well maybe a forklift or a flat bed truck aw
na'll ya'll it's my fault that I'm stuck...

Midnight rendezvous with Wendy's' menu's, watching TV
not much else I can do but eat and sleep and here I will lye...
until mom brings over some of her hot apple pie!
..and don't forget the milk ya'll to wash it all down!

My stomach hurts my face is frowned but I can't stop I must relate about all of the food that I just ate.

Got to go, got to go got to make room for some more. Off to the bathroom don't you know!

Mm –Mm- Mm...
By LMJ

The Bar-B-Q...

Fatback slab, baby back ribs potato salad,
babies dressed in colorful bibs.
Music playing underneath the sun, loud laughter
fills the park and slow dances in the dark,

Watermelon, spaghetti, corn on the cob, greens,
baked beans, macaroni and cheese...
Screams set off by buzzing bees...

Softball, volleyball, ice cream and cake
looking for more pictures to take...
Jump rope, singing and dance contest, wet
t-shirts from squirting water guns...
Families having fun in the sun...

Visitors, fiancés, husbands and wives children playing, cousins having
the time of their lives...

Snoozing in a breeze in the shade...
Under the trees people laid...

Car lights, car horns on in the park...
Playing cards, listening to soft blues in the dark...
Strolling back and forth down memory lane...
Listening to the engines of over head airplanes...

Packing up now, food to take home, kissing and
hugging goodbye the children start to
Moan... ah, what a great day we all had...

Starting out with fatback slab, baby back ribs, potato salad, watermelon,
baked beans, spaghetti, corn on the cob, greens, macaroni and cheese
quieted the sound of the buzzing bees...

At the Bar-B-Q.

By LMJ

JUDGMENT DAY

I went to God and prayed
Told him it was my soul I wish he'd save
Told him that I no longer wanted to be a slave

He told me he'd wash me clean
Give me life in abundance that and love like I'd never seen
He held me and washed me
He comforted me and told me things would be alright
Now I have no more sleepless nights

My dreams are large and so is my heart
I do intend to leave them impart
To you, these simple but kind words to guide you through

Go to God and pray
He'll wash your sins away
Cast them into the sea of forgetfulness
Your soul he'll surely bless

Now that isn't to say
That trouble won't come your way
As sure as the sky is blue
The devil will come after you

But hold fast to that which is good
You'll find your name in the great book
That book you think you live today, NO
But the book used on judgment day

He's done it for me; he'll do it for you
He has no respect of person and no one to answer to

Go on, God cares for you
Go on, he will see you through
Go on, he will make a way out of no way
Go on, he will. But you must obey
Go on...

I'll see you on judgment day!

LMJ

For Michael Dampier
Missing since: 9/3/2004

Our Children…

Our children have gone missing
In cold graves used and abused or sold as slaves…

Our children have gone missing
Walking the streets
Long winter night sleeps in abandoned buildings
Or in back of empty car seats

Our children…

Our children have gone missing
While some pariah, predator and pedophile
Has something to prove…

Our children have gone missing
1-800-THE-LOST and the National Center
for Missing and Exploited
Children are pressing the issue…

Our children have gone missing
With alerts that flash all over the TV
AMBER ALERT…on the sides of roads
Blinking. Blinking… and questions asked
#1 being: It's 10 O'clock,
DO YOU KNOW WHERE YOUR CHILDREN ARE?

Our children have gone missing
And war is raging
And yet the headline reads,
"Madonna adopts David a Malawian boy."

Famine, Aids/HIV, War and poverty, Drugs,
Rape, Violence, Tears Greed and pain
What will be left for our children to gain?

Our children have gone missing
…and where are we? Voices be strong even if you must SCREAM
`Cause…

Our children…
Have gone missing!

Are you listening?
Can you hear me?

By LMJ

Did you feel that God?

I know that it was you
You, he who has made me
While reading in the bible, record of your deeds
How you moved things
Made things happen
Worked them all together for the good
The good of your glory that men may tell the story
Forever and a day

I felt the awe of you the pure spine tingling
Blood curdling mind blowing awesomeness of
You, running through my body

As I read of Joseph in the book of genesis
As in every book
I am touched of you
Reminded that my God
Is an awesome God

As I have felt you
You have felt me
You have heard my prayers and my thoughts in silence
My tears and fears are not strangers to you
You have seen the good and the unclean things that I have done
And still you have loved me
Unconditionally

You have known me from the very beginning
It's no wonder that men sit in fear of the future
For not knowing you
The unseen and the unfamiliar
There's no faith

Did you feel that God?
Did you feel me feeling you?
Quickening of your spirit lay to my flesh
On the inside
Running through me
A charge
To seek you
To trust you
To love you
And I do…

My dreams had been shortened
My heart had been broken
And my spirit and soul had been crushed
Stripped away

I didn't think I'd see the light of day
And I really didn't care to
And then came you…

Rescuing me from myself
And I just want to say thank you,

Thank you God.

By LMJ

It's over…

I'm remembering the day at the park
In the car
In the broad day light we stroked

I lay still thinking about the dreams we shared
….what was said just between us

My love went away
He's not planning to come back anytime soon

The way he smiles
The excitement in his step
The hurt
The love
The pain
The separation
The disbelief
The disdain
The smell of his cologne
The remembrance of our favorite songs

I'm remembering the day in the bedroom
Our first time

The music played
..and we danced

I pray for the pain to go away
But it lingers

I thought
We had
Something

When will it be over?
Me
Remembering
Me
Wanting him
Me
Still being in love with…
My first love

By LMJ

The pain that floods my soul...

The pain that floods my soul
Burns and hurts spins me into an evolution
No where listed in the constitution
Under life and the pursuit of happiness
Was a stylistic portrait of me

Yeah I'm stressed
Mind bent
I confess that this here game called life hurts
Burns and leaves me yearning for yet
Another turn
Another chance
...To try

I've given up on asking the reasons why... to a point
Until I come up with a new joint
Now I just wonder when
When... will... I... be... free?
How do I escape to just be me?

Quick clichés of seemingly smarter then me folk
Have ran their course,
All over my head and still I
Am left with these burns,
These hurts and pains
I say evolution cause I know this has got evolve into
Something!

When it's quiet it's loud and when it's loud I ache and ache
Cause I just aint where want to be but I heard
somewhere that I'm right where I'm suppose to be,
This is what I feel
So don't you go telling me I can't have feelings
Cause it's too late

Say a prayer?

My knees are black and my tears have fallen, my
Hands have been folded and my arms have been out stretched,
My face has been in the floor and my head held down,
My mouth has been dry; dry to the point of sleep
My tears have turned into whimpers
For there is nothing left
I... am... spent

Oh, the pain that floods my soul!
It's a wonder my blood hasn't begun to boil
My heart hasn't busted
From these pains of being
Discussed with my life

Constitute this... Construct that... Create this
I confirm this bliss- less- ness
that a change is going to come? What? NO
Has to come!

Change?
...I have
...I will
...I can
...I am...
I am...
Evolving from
This pain
This hurt that
Encourages me... to live
My soul just won't let it be

This still doesn't stop the feeling
Cause I'm still alive
I won't feel anything when I die...
and it won't matter then.

By LMJ

Barack OBAMA…08

Collectively we watched his-story being made
As a black man turned from prisoner and slave,
decade after decade…after decade
Into…

The president of the United States…Of America…

No color just sound
No chains…but freedom…

His-story and Her-story will be told and not
only about how a nation was sold
Separated, hung, raped, hosed down beaten and spit in their faces
And told to take their places…at the back of the bus

The revolution done been televised…and will continue to be
Even before and after a King having a Dream…

No color just sound
No chains…but freedom…

To the young with no one to look to for strength and courage
For the young person afraid of the world and its gifts
For the old caught up in past myths
Watch how the tide shifts…it shifts
To the oppressed, distressed and confused
Torn, worn, beaten down and misused…

The revolution done been televised…

Your skin my skin…
**Black or white is the only thing written
on between pen and paper,**
Your life my life…
**Black or white is the only thing written
on between pen and paper,**

**No color just sound
No chains…but freedom…**
…and the country knew, we needed him… we needed him…

…BARACK… (The Vote)

**No color just sound
No chains…but freedom…**

to have hope…to have something to believe again…cause we had been
spent to the red white and blue matter of having to circumvent…
and air our dirty laundry all over this great country…with the call
for a stimulus…check one two check…one selves to find the sum of
reason…

Reasons why we as a people must come together… come together,

**No color just sound
No chains…but freedom…**

…And oh it rings… it rings,

**No color just sound
No chains…but freedom…**

His-story…Her-story…Your-story…Our-story
Has been and will continue to be televised and collectively
We are the revolution…

By LMJ

Give me the ugly...

With so many other things to think about or do without the temporal
most would think before looking and except before adoration…
…but in the middle of these truths in the
rawness of the ugly we find reality

Yours and mine

Is it not in the ugly that we find ourselves from weakness to strength?
…made whole
Is it not by weakness to strength that we find ourselves purified?
In stead of full of pride…lost and embryonic souls
Or where… oh where and how… can we break the fall
doth the cradle break?
at the least we know

I have looked in on beauty and seen evil there
I have looked past the ugly to my despair
to have to look again

Um…

In the eye…?
yea, they told me
beauty was in the eye of the beholder
…but whose looking
and is there a reflection there…
stemming from the eye that dares to look
 …is it mirrored…tapered or in full glare
cry loud aloud
spare me not

Give me the ugly, the raw…
spare not at my expense
give me the truth!
that I may grow…
that I may be full
and…
whole

By LMJ

Love me past my pain…

Dare me to live again in loves sweet bosom
Rap me in your love and spoil me with your attentiveness
Wet my Pilate of desire
Shower me with your thoughts of me
Cleave to me
Want and need me
Take me…now

I implore you
Be my knight and shinning armor
Ruffle the petals of this passed over flower
And rain on me

Let the drizzles from your wet moist being
Fall on me… into me… and around me

Lay thick upon my heart and impart your wisdom there
Show me your majesties
Live rent free in my mind…sweetly

Touch my soul with godly love
Fold into me with all that you are and rest there
Edify my longing for knowledge of who you are
And tease me not

Drain and refresh me daily
Call me sweet names…
Darling
Honey
Sugar
Baby
Lover
Friend

Lean
Long and
Lay…
Rent and be spent
Of your self…completely

Dance with me
Laugh with me
Cry with me
Never withholding your strength
Share my life and my bed
I say yes…

Apply pleasure as needed

I am a dreamer
Dream with me
Produce with me
Be my partner
Loudly and boldly with content

Are you near?
Can you feel me?
Do you ache for me as I ache for you?
Take me
Caress me through to the insides
Bless me with your entirety

Find me whole
Find me now
And love me past
My pain

…I am waiting
for you…

The flower that I love...

The smell...
the essence of this lingering piece of perfection
lit with colors only an adoring eye dare see,
lying here next to me

the aroma intoxicates me
takes me higher
makes me feel full

I drink and eat of its purity
oh, how I'd love to hold this flower in my arms
caressing it's petals...freely

smiles of beauty
smells of earth and rain refreshed of all that is good and natural

lays on you...thick
...and rested

Oh, this flower
this remarkable piece of beauty
this enchanted gift from God
this wondrous mystery

...has smitten me
I take time, I take reason and engulf the opportunity
with loving senses... with my arms and hold...

...the flower that I love

By LMJ

Inspired by..rock3, lit

Disintegrated dreams…

Why what do you mean disintegrated dreams?

…Well you know exactly what I mean…

The dreams of a young girl pregnant; with all that she dare dream for a future unseen but hoped for…in her mind, then she becomes unconcerned and unalarmed of her potential and her own worth that she gives birth by lying on her back…and know she can only dream for the child she has to raise…alone

Why what do you mean disintegrated dreams, well look a here , look a here…that man, that wo-man so caught up and lost in his or her fears that he/she drinks it all down…smokes it all up and ends up in jail he/she done gave up…

His/her prayer reads; what the hell might as well…sell sell sell and settle for less cause he/she aint worried about Sundays' best and scriptures or hymns…

So he/she spends-he/she spends himself/herself into a frenzy thinking about what he/she could've been and what done happened already… cause he's/she's scared fear done gripped him/her to his/her soul…the boy/girl the man/wo-man child done been spoiled…

letting some man/woman carry him on her/his back…

What do I mean disintegrated dreams?

Yours…

Stand on your own…God gave you the authority to!

The future has a past...

The future has a past
and he who laughs last
laughs last...laughs last

yeah and that would be me
laughing...

went on a trip yesterday
seen my past through fresh eyes
and to my surprise, yep I'm still here
laughing...

pushed past some obstacles and jumped, kneeled, crawled and ran over
some hurdles I've even cursed the day I was born...um, a few times

mind blown to bits and back
shook in trembles of desperation
evaluating life's situations that:
I, me myself has gotten in... And out of

Yeah and that would be me laughing...now
cause it sure as hell wasn't funny then

Yeah...

He who laugh last laughs last laughs last
...yep, that would be me...

...laughing!

...happy about my future and grateful for making it through my past

Flip it.

By LMJ

Where are you
My love

…I'm waiting
Waiting for you to push my hair back behind
my ear and kiss me deeply on my neck
So deeply that I have to do a panty check
Cause I'm moist
…and you say: it's alright, I'm here
Moist with thoughts of you touching my soul and me:
tasting the knowledge on the tip of my tongue that you so
eloquently put down in such a vibrant motion with respect
Oh yeah, verbs the word
I have been able to see inside of your mind
through other senses and you blow me
…I'm waiting
The stimulation is a paramount and never ends
Times after time you spend me until I am completely spent
…and limp ooo- baby- baby I have given you
all of me and have received you fully
…and you say: it's alright I'm here
Pulling me up with your strength and taking me to mountains
and plains that meet the sky and as the sun melts into the darkness
I watch as the stars dance above your head and I breathe
…softly and gently
I'm happy and you?
you're here and it's true,
it's alright

Is anybody out there?

Isolation…

I sit here not knowing and wondering and wishing, hoping and clinging to what may and could be…looking for the better part of me to show up…

I'm watching life go on around me waiting for my turn
you see I'm doing the best that I can…

Plans? yeah I've got plans and goals and dreams and yes
they're written down…you know to make them more
real so that I can actually visualize my dreams…
however scary it may seem…I want to live

I wake up in the morning and I thank god for the life he has given me
however unfair it may seem to be…because I want to live and I look
forward to living better, being better giving better…seeing better

I routinely gather my senses and rebuke with all of the defenses that I
have inside of me the thoughts of negativity…just to make it through
the day…and the night, the nights…

They are lonely and bold, they peer at me pointing at the empty spots…
there in my heart, my life, my bed …and I ache

I dream of writing about love and happy connections
and knights in shinning armors
trees and lilies, romance and the divine ways of
making love…physically and mentally
but I am not there…not yet

My prize my constellation is in knowing that hopefully at the end on
the day…I'll know myself better and that better part of me will have
shown up…well at least that's what I tell myself anyway

Jonas…Daniel…Samson…Ezekiel…Job…Elijah…Peter and me
fate, destiny…

Hello…is anybody out there?
can you feel me?

By LMJ

Prove it to yourself...

The person you used to be
Isn't the person you now see,
Way back when they were telling you stuff like:

This isn't you; this is not how I brought you up
Come on now enough is enough!

You can change people change all of the time...
Start acting like that child of mine,
Sister of mine, brother of mine, mother of mine

...and then you go and blow their minds
You, change...

Don't look for the trust to be there or for
them to treat you with respect
They'll tell you: you haven't earned it yet...

It could be one year, two maybe three...
Well let's face it, it may not ever be

Thing is you have now become you
And even though you've done what they've asked you to
Doesn't mean that they will be here for you
Believe in you
Come around you
Include you
...they my even say that they support and
Love you...
Just don't expect them to...

It's your life so what are you going to do?
I'll tell you what you're going to do:
You're going to rise above the hurt and pain
God has blessed you to live again

You're going to formulate a plan
You can do it I know that you can
There will be some lonely nights…
And sometimes things won't go just right,
You'll cry and feel hurt and pain
..But let me tell you there is no shame,
…In living…
Soon the victory you'll be winning

I have learned, that's why I'm giving
Confidence and words of inspiration to you!
It's your time,
God will see you through
You can win!
Prove it to yourself…
Cause **I know that you can!**

Single Parents…

God Bless single parents, let me just first say!

One income that's barely an income
One job to get to before the break of dawn
One me, one you to spread among:
Creditors
Bill collectors that may as well collect our bones
…and what about robbing Peter to pay Paul
when you don't even know who they are?

Have I gotten your attention thus far?
Wave your hands if you're a single parent
because I know you can relate
…and no one to fix you a hot plate, draw you a bath or speak sweet
words into your ear, massage your neck, your back… during and before
the aftermath…

You working by your self, bill paying, on your knees praying, lunch
toting, got to be playing games with the baby after work dragging,
sweet smile having through the falling rain non-umbrella having, back
riding child support non-receiving because the daddy done gone and
started another family? and aint believing that his day is coming that
he will have to pay the piper…woooooo, all while trying to decipher
the hit's and misses on any given list in this here game called life!….
your move…

Shall I persist?

Yes, yes…God Bless the single parents well maintained mother's role
because we're just about the only ones who have the hearts and souls to
do this job…and do it well, like a ship with out a sale and Eve without
an Adam not that we wish not to have him, we just want for him to
stay around without all of the drama…and they have the nerves to talk
about baby mama's…

Woooooo, I'm gonna back away from that one…but you know!

Juggle this, that and the other thing, prayer in the evening for what the next day may bring…say it aint so! Say it aint so! …Yeah, it's so… and it's a sadly excepted blow that our young ones must face…

Absent parents take your place…TAKE YOUR PLACE face the music and dance…dance I said! Instead of hopping in and out of beds when you've got children that need to be; housed, clothed educated and fed… hum may as well be a crack head…

…Cause you sure do have crack head like tendencies!
…so what the hook gone be?

I sure hope its papa's got a brand new bag cause that old one he keeps popping out of sucks!

Too Proud, Too Free...

From Africa to plantations and traveling towards freedom
by way of Underground Railroad stations, and nightly
visitations from old master breaking the bloodline
After being raped mentally and physically this
is what the end result would be...
Young, old and the past lives and deaths of slaves sold by the white of
their teeth the step in their stride and the yolks of their eyes... a people
filled with pride, kings... queens prince and princesses, were dethroned
shackled and placed in bondage and ripped from their families and
homes and commanded to forget their own...heritage...language and
urged to forget about gaining knowledge...and whipped to except it.

For years and decades African Americans were taught to
hide in the shadows of shades, walk and talk with their
heads hung low no up right greetings of hello...
yesa maser nosa maser you'd hear in an unforgotten echo

...and this is what the end result would be...

Were beaten, hung, mutilated, castrated and degraded...I'm talking
mental, emotional, inhumane anguish, BUT that which was first and
made last shall be first again...

From the backs of buses, to driving the buses
From living in the projects to building great homes
From crack house's to counseling in prestigious counseling offices
From jails to becoming a judge
From being counted out for the color of our skin to being counted on
from working at the backstairs of the white house to running the white
house in government and of course: CHANGE

The end result has yet to reach it's full potential for there are still sick and suffering individuals that are stuck in the past where speaking and laughing with ours heads held high and being free still reproaches the very skin and thoughts that ride in on their little minds as if it were the air they owned and breath…

Except it, learn it, like it, live it and love it!

With this in mind: if it were not for the predecessors I could not, would not be able to write, breath, speak, dance, love, laugh in freedom with my head held high nor could you… so know that you can.

Hold up your head look your counter parts in their eyes and smile that wondrous smile that God gave you, it's yours, cover not your talents for they are the source of your livelihood, explore the world through books and take flight…

Grow and plant new seeds…live out your dreams and fantasies even if some people don't like other people being…too proud or too free, we're really not crabs in a barrel…

…and I sigh, in hopes that you will live, laugh, dance and love with your heads held high! cause it's a new day Boss!

Lady in waiting…

Hum… as I retract the memories of my mind and find that I am standing, laying sitting, breathing, eating and living alone, I exhale wooooooooooooo and I remember… I recall what it was like being connected to someone…

…and I long, I long to feel that I am running across someone's mind and invading their thoughts pleasantly and that in the exact thought; a smile or a pleasurable shiver creeps up their spine along side of tingles just enough to make them lick their lips and reach for the telephone…

I'm here and I am waiting to feel real to be acknowledged with hugs and kisses oh how I miss them, with sweet touches and kind words, along side of needful deeds…

Aiming to please me as I am willing to please him…in such a way

I've seen his silhouette in my minds eye and
he is handsome strong and beautiful
Caressing more then my body but taking me
into his spirit as our souls connect,
For this…I am waiting but not just waiting…
praying and anticipating his arrival

Saying things like:

God ready me for this journey
Teach me how to love this man
Guide my lips as well as my steps
Keep me from my self and create in me whom
you will have me be for him-
by your design…

Oh I pray…

I pray for him, for his walk with God and his ability to love me in the way that God would have a man love a woman…completely and respectfully

…and I wonder, I wonder if God is preparing him for me as he has prepared Eve for Adam, and again I pray that the mistakes we make not weigh heavy as those left by them

I seek God's will and listen for his choice, his voice and
his plan for my life as this man's future wife…
…yet, I wonder because he's not here and I want for him to be

I want to make love knowing that god is happy with each touch of me freely giving of myself without my bed being defiled, I want to bask in God's glory and rest in my man's arms forever drinking him in… drinking him in, without sin

For this I'll wait…I'll wait
Who is he? Where he is…Lord show me, tell me… better yet tell him!

Stop this ride…I want OFF!

This see-saw, this merry-go-round…

Ever feel like you want get off…
get off… just to exhale what the hell I may as well tell, although I know we've all got stories to tell but you ain't me… so I'm going to tell mine…

No this ain't no ordinary rhyme…so sorry; life can be a bit scary at times… it might just be a nightmare…

Ain't no shake and bake…I'm talking slithering, slippery, predatory snakes from past to present tense, damn this hellish freaknic ain't no walk in the park or sandy shores it ain't **even** a picnic…it's hell bent…

BUT…I'm tired tired to the point of being inspired to flow in this direction, I'm not looking for any constellation prizes or kisses neither nor hugs not even protection, I'm just looking for a way… OFF THIS RIDE…

Let me start this trip so you don't slip and you'll know just what I'm talking about…

creepy seedy men the ones with the sheepish grins and tight eyed looks running side ways from the corners of their eyes with everything ugly and vile hidden inside, behind storied smiles these calculated… predatory pedophiles…

from victims themselves they learned to dispel the ever growing monster festering inside… creeping in and out of seeping thoughts that grew into demonic acts of beastly genocide… no longer the same little boys casting aside there young bright toys for natural use they grew tired, Ah… but to play with young and innocent little girls…somehow they felt inspired…

I know I know you saying what in the world!

YES IN THIS WORLD...

My sentiments exactly... and in the church no less could or would this pedophile be... lets back this thing up cause YES-OH-YES I'm stressed and putting it down! I got to get my Ill off and this is the only way that I know how...

So let me...

corners...locked doors or cars odd places never explored... behind... underneath...in coat closets or in the chapel seats... in the dark out of reach...out of reach for the help that each child needs...

that's where you'll find this leech, this freak... he or she could look as you or I... lays back cool for he or she's no fool... could be looking right at you... there, in your face an ordinary yet so unordinary waiting... waiting to take his prey...

Burning...I feel it just like it was yesterday... freshly I can see him not seeing me watching what he looked like as he left me...on the chapel seat, fear gripping me ever weak this child I use to be...
...and again this spirit re-visited me... by visiting my child... this pedophile, this pedophile reached past and beyond me...

Reached out to touch a flower so innocent and lovely for as much as purity in this here world will allow...UGGGGGGGGGOD!

STOP THIS RIDE I WANT OFF...

I toss and turn burn and yearn to learn inside how a person could walk past their pride... and hold their heads up high, after committing such a treacherous act of genocide...HELL...WHY...HOW...

You low belly crawling, unconcerned about who's future you're robbing, back stabbing, unadulterated kid snatch riding...rubbing...grind-bump grubbing, unrealistic host of a human being, con-artist-driving, self gratifying, unstructured, insecure, resemblance of life...you dirty nasty dog... HOW could you and WHY...

Your card has been peeped you in the hole (the pit) YO... and this isn't it, it's not enough! It's NOT enough...your cover is about to be BLOWN....BLOWN to HELL it's time... it's time you know, it's time...

Whoever you are...OH and YOU KNOW...HOW DARE YOU...HOW DARE YOU...HOW COULD YOU... touch a child?

Have faith in God...Watch the world...BUT...keep your eyes on your children.

Mom…Dad …I'm gay…

Someone touched my poodie pie, my wee wee
I've been abused,
I was curious but misused
And then…
I liked it and couldn't stop
So now…I'm happy about it,
I'm just gay about it…

My pain has been turned into pleasure although it may hurt you.
I'm gay…this is my life, my decision…my uphill battle that just might
come crashing down but let me take this toll,

I'll pay for it…in change… or it'll be rent out of my hide
But no longer can I hold inside
The confines of my mind
My minds content of being different
So what if I must fight for the rest of my life
To hold hands with a man or woman…the same as me
Getting silent stares of disapproval compared to living
A life of secrecy
Was brutal…for me
Faced the possibility of being beaten or killed
Wondering about God's will…for me
Wearing stamps of approvals
T-shirts that proudly read
Gay-pride
And parades that fade after marching into the TV news

Back then I couldn't tell you…
Mom… dad…someone touched my poodie pie or my wee wee
So I found content of what my young mind
thought life was supposed to be
Not the opposite of what I thought I must hide…
…In a closet…
Mom…Dad finally…

Someone touched my poodie pie...my wee wee
So now...I'm gay.

Now I walk around screaming with pride...
Am I happy though?
Because that's what gay really means

Find your peace.

By LMJ

Shop Closed…

This other woman trauma drama
You know the one that you tried to put me through
Well I ain't going boo…

You say; I'm just talking to her for business,
she got my and I need my...
Never mind that she'll call me later
Cause if I can't be here and get catered then maybe
Just maybe I'll just be back with you later

No feelings, no ideas, no heart, no self control
Hell I don't think I even got a soul
No lip, no expressions no long drawn out questions
Just do, say, be
Whatever I say is convenient?
For me

That's what you say…
Let me do you a solid and give it to straight away
You aren't going to break my heart, my pockets, my spirit, my soul
Listen boo I'm in control
I–got- this
So there,
No bodies moves no body gets hurt
What you say…
I'm not one to suffer
I do what's convenient for me
From pillow to post, yeah that's where you'll find me
So what ever I have to do I will do
No time to make commitments to you
It's not you, baby it's me
 My roots aren't broken but I fled from the wise tree
Ain't no crime in doing me

Well...
Find some one else to cater to you
Shop closed! Yeah I' talking to you
You pride less
Trying to be self centered
Still got some growing up to do
You 40 year old promising what you will and won't do
Dressed up garbage can...
I don't need you I wants me a real MAN!
...I Got- to- go, see you when I see you!

I'm waiting…

waiting for you to push my hair back behind my ear and kiss me deeply
on my neck so deeply that I have to do a panty check,
cause I'm moist…

…and you say: it's alright, I'm here

moist with thoughts of you touching my soul and me: tasting the
knowledge on the tip of my tongue that you so eloquently put down in
such a vibrant motion with respect

oh yeah, verbs the word

I have been able to see inside of your mind through other senses and
you blow me

…I'm waiting

The stimulation is paramount and never ends
time after time you spend me until I am completely spent

… and limp ooo- baby- baby I have given you
all of me and have received you fully

…and you say: it's alright I'm here

Pulling me up with your strength and taking me to mountains and
plains that meet the sky and as the sun melts into the darkness I watch
as the stars dance above your head and I breathe

…softly and gently

I'm happy and you?
You're here and it's true,
it's alright

By LMJ

Battery...

Thought you were a regular man; beautiful, funny, charismatic and charming the very definition of what a prince would be...

Until the day you beat me quiet little words unbeknown to me would be the start of the abuse...verbally.

Flowers, candy presents and that charm that you appear to be so full of like a light switch you turn it on and off...off and on with me waiting never knowing in the dark how or when you'll change...not knowing when the switch is on...or off for that matter waiting for the spark...
So I left thinking or hoping you'd find something or someone else to occupy that gaping hole some how held up inside of you but you didn't you came after me time after time...How is a mother to raise a daughter/son in a world without fear, without prejudice when the very person said to love would be the very person to hurt or kill us...Kill our lives or dreams and hopes for a normal future and comfort of family what of the men/women she/he would chose to have in her/his life would they beat her/him would she/he allow it to be so because she/he thinks ok because it's what she/he has seen you do to me,

I live in fear of these questions, I explain it to my mind and I left her/him up in prayer...I know that as time goes on I will be strong enough to guide her/him through whatever the need be for I am a survivor and so shall she/he be...

Corrupt, mangled and twisted inside the only thing holding you together is your foolish pride... and the devil is breaking you speaking evil of me into your ear it's not love that he speaks when you hurt and beat me repeatedly... it's hate and fear because secretly you live there right along with him in your mind...I pray for your redemption.

Leave and pray...pray while leaving...please don't stay you deserve she/he deserves a chance in life to be free...

If it's a boy what will he be, will he be the same woman beater that he's grown to know as a child full of anger, rage and the ugliness of being hostile....**so unnecessary...**We all must choose our own roads but when we chose for ourselves and our children it will be what they know...nurture them, teach them right from wrong and help lead and guide them to grow...with a sound mind minus the fear speak words of wisdom and life into their ears...

To battery we say **no**, to hate and reproach we say **no**, to fear and confusion we say **no**, to living a life of bondage we say **no**, to being the jump to start your battery **we say NO...To life, love and the pursuit of happiness we say...YES**
We will give ourselves a chance...

Love & light Queens...LMJ.

We've stopped…

We've stopped believing in fairytales and dreams
The world has become so desensitized it seems
Fairies and magic has turned into dust
Replaced with video's and lust
Gun shots and mayhem stand in dreams way
Of what a child dare dream of becoming some day

The days of Willie Wonka and his chocolate factory
Of Peter pan and Wendy of doctor's and lawyer's and husband and
wives have been replaced with pimps, prostitutes and dope fiends and
gangland terrorist by no surprise

So it seems…

Video's collaged with big chains and naked girls have stolen the precious
fantasies of our young ones and have been replaced with baggy pants
and bothersome chants of debased ballads for what is now called
music… invades us so deep to the point of no sugar plums dancing
above sleeping heads and fairytale dreams as our children sleep…they
sleep,

They sleep to the world and it's jagged edged possibilities, they're dreams
have been murdered and it's no real mystery, all you have to do is turn
on the TV and dreams vanish, play a video game and dreams vanish,
listen to the iPod all day and they…vanish hanging out with the wrong
crowds…they vanish in a world that's busy… busy turning the dime
and calculating futures into turning green… and time shares…where
are they? The people who care? Some say they are rich without despair
but for inner city youth there's nothing but the blues no dreams, no
fantasies, no sugar plums or fairytales with happy endings…

Whose dreams vanish
Whose life stagnant
Whose promises'
Broken

Whose suffering
The token
The token
Products of their environment

A band and bland of misguided raw and sometimes savage energy
Has become the battle that our children see,
not knowing fully what they seek
They listen and watch the communities of which
they share, some are shell shocked
Some escape with minor scrapes and bruises
some have become future abusers

We've stopped…
Believing and sharing our dreams thinking
about how petty they may seem
In essence we've prevented the growth of young
minds, of future kings and queens
Because we've allowed it to be so
Knowledge turned backwards? …In short… stupefied.
Lost in beats, tire wheels and drugs without prescription… guns and jail
cells and eventually prison there's nothing left but death after that…

Tell me how can we get them back, get them back…answer me!
Lost in crowds these painful faces
Living in lost and lonely silent places
Needles…mmm
Pipes…mmm
Bottles…mmm
Sex…mmm
Power by selling to the nations supposed rejects…mmm

Fairytale, wishes, and caviar dreams
Muffled by substitutions that pretend to bring solace, quieted are the
screams with a pacifier…an imitation…a lie

Rape and violation carries into latter shame filled with promiscuous actions tangled in regrets… and fear, fear of life in a world so determined not to show…

The prolific and profound undermining of a generations future… lost, loss of dreams, fairytales, wishes and happy endings… love, education and the certifiable admission of said loss

We've stopped believing
We must start again
If the future is to have a chance
As adults we could look through our children's eyes
We could ask for a clean heart
Wisdom, knowledge and of course understanding
In order to find faith hope and belief
In the gift of love, life and dreams

Look to your children
Remember, gain total recall
We use to be them,
And what did we want
What did we need
Who heard us
What went wrong

Lions, tigers and bears…
Oh, me.
Oh my.

By LMJ

Lost innocence...

Creeping you crept while innocence slept
Slithering you filtered into my room
Wearing the disguise of a loved one
You were trusted too soon...too soon
Stealing you stole what did not belong to you
No...there were no obvious bruises to show nothing black and blue
At least not on the outside...

Years went past but wounds ran deep
with unspoken thoughts or words of what you did to me
Did you not know how deep you'd send me when you stole?
When you sold your soul for a piece of me
That had not been given...freely

Long nights on end I tossed and I turned
Never knowing the degrees of my inward burns
I viewed every man differently...
...classmates, teachers, the organist... way--aay down to the preacher
any man...and in some cases I found that I was right to be

Do I submit...do I give before they take from me...?
Do I follow a life of promiscuity 'cause some girls do after dealing with
a so called man with the likes of you

**I had no idea or clue of what my life was supposed to be or what it
would become**

My thoughts were twisted my mind confused
I was used...I was used... I had been abused
Seeming never to understand the limitations
of what was supposed to be
How to act or to be around a man I felt
uncomfortable in my own skin
but what I later found to be true was that it was not supposed to be

…you creeping, creep creature stealing from me…laying with me… touching me…threatening me making sex with a man a dirty thing,

Was it a tool, a weapon, or a gift…a promise of
love given in marriage and morality?
For procreation or sheer ecstasy…pain for women
and pleasure for men or an alleged, I searched for
the answers…again and again and again…

With silent stares and tense glares because you knew just like me
who, why and what you had done to me… when I
looked into your eyes these few words they use to
haunt me…who do you think she'll believe…
This thief, stealing…creeping…slithering, slippery vile male
wanna be, wearing the disguise of family…put his hands on me

I slipped and slid in and out of confusion misled and did as most women did, I bit my lip and hid behind something… pushed it all way--aay down deep… covered my pain with smiles mask and sheets and in turn I folded into the cold self storage of myself and watched my life pass me by, in fiery colors and deep shades of grey…

Yeah I showed up in increments but even then I wasn't there.

I'll say no names because you know just who you be
But if you're reading this…then it's you that's feeling me…
I got my hands on you…
I'm not biting my lip
I've got a strong grip now!

I no longer have to tell…God knows
…and he's going to get you!

LMJ

Truth be told…

I wrote down my feelings because there was no one to trust with them
and I could write down how I felt better then if they poured or spewed
heavily from my lips. Or just maybe the people that I've trusted became
tired of listening. It is my prayer that you'll listen because after reading
my poems some time later myself I found reason and purpose of all
of the unanswered questions in my life and healing in letting out the
pain from the disastrous paths I had chosen to take…purpose. Pen and
paper had become relative to me, my life line. I didn't know how to
make sense of anything, my mind had been spent and my heart broken
over life and the reason that I had to live it with out even wanting to
bared down on me.

So…I wrote. I wrote to the sounds of the beating
pains that rang inside of my soul
I wrote for the voice that I could not be for myself…aloud
I wrote to tare down
I wrote to build up
I wrote to escape
I wrote to dream
I wrote of becoming and living
I wrote in the silence of walls, in the
midnight hours of sleepless nights
I prayed, I cried and I wrote without even knowing that I could.

I have never sat down to write with intent, the words come and
sometimes I'm not certain if the word that's there is correct in its use.
It takes no time to get them down and afterwards I come to find that
everything is as it should be…isn't God amazing?

Read, question, write, dream, eat, drink, love
and live to the glory of God why?
Because in all that he has done it has been for his
glory that men may serve and honor him.

I pray for the edification of your mind and spirit.

This sistah speaks…

What has happened?

…Am I wrong to believe that true love exist?
When it seems that a world so big on ideas has some how forgotten about love and commitment, was it all just an illusion to want that special person with whom you can connect? As apposed to just someone to hook up with…

I've been watching from the outside looking in at marriages and supposed partnerships and they are all at risk of ending unexpectedly, scary huh? Married men want their cake and pie…married women don't mind dating somebody else's guy…these days it goes both ways…

Role reversals:
Lioness have become cougars
Queens's have been broken down to ordinary hood rats
Men have reverted to being little boys
A woman to woman encounter
A male to male encounter
Not so unordinary these days…

I want to believe, I want to believe that there is a man out there waiting for me, looking for me…waiting for every little princess; her prince… for every Queen her King, match point…

I'm at a cross road, and I'm trying to save myself, I'm not bad looking, I'm funny and smart and I can admit to not knowing it all, I am both lover and friend ambitious for an ideal quality of life that's adorned with its many possibilities…I can talk about what I use to be where I've been and who I hope to become…openly and honestly,

I am not afraid… guilt and shame no longer lives here…

I have kissed them deeply and open heartedly, I've shared my bed my dreams and my fears, I have related to them on levels that I have yet relate with a true man and oh how I long to, I have had constant battles in my mind and open cries have stained my pillow for such a live and blessed connection of the opposite section of life…a lovely man

I want to wake to the smell of fresh manliness and rest in the arms of absolution, I want to connect like lego blocks and smile like Miss Ceilee after a nights session with shug, I'd like for him to carry me in his heart, soul, mind, body and spirit…

Question is… does this exist? Am I a fool
to want something like this?
Is this a notion that I should quietly dismiss?
Nowadays everything is so quick so filled with convenience all the way down to the vagina and penis… those two words use to mean something now they are just words used at doctors' visits… easily replaced by dick and pussy, and I thought Dick was a man's name and pussy was a cat…

I'm trying to save myself, this woman speaks…are you listening?
Edification and companionship is a blessing and I feel deep with in me that I'm missing…missing…

A honey dip surprise, fuck buddy, maintenance man or
woman, somebody else's guy…NO I want my own!
Midnight conversations on the phone,
Smiles at first glance, feeling him from my head, heart, stomach… to my vagina through to my toes…feeling myself explode inside myself in incomplete shivers of awe…Um Um Um…oooh…

Tell me do you, do you have any clue of how a
real woman feels a man? …Completely.
Still waters run way…deep, more then inches more then check books and pays stubs, hub caps and crazy sexy cool duds…hair does and hair cuts, materialistic it is not… just the mere mentioning of the word love has a domino effect…and one that we should all respect because it's God as he has commanded it.

…It is so

Not something to be bridled or controlled, sifted
or sold it is a gift to be given away
For it is the only way you'll ever keep it…

This sister speaks…are you listening?

By LMJ

Criminal Background Resume

Objective

To show you the difference an ex-drug dealing, crack head/dope fiend can make in a world that has some how counted them out.

Work Experience

Dealer/Thief/crack head/dope fiend
Drug infestation Inc. For Money
The Greater Chicago Land Area

Description:

To buy drugs at a wholesale price, cut down, bag up and distribute, to stay as far away from the police as possible.

To maintain a personal and customer service friendly report within neighboring communities that housed crack heads and dope fiends.

To keep my own people sleep and affected without knowing the devastating and harsh realities of the out come by trying to get ahead.

Accomplishments:

- sold the highest in record sales for a non-gang related dealer
- recruited other sales personnel for a less then moderate pay rate
- kept most crack heads and dope fiends in line
- Stopped the possibilities of my future and those around me

Education

School or Program Name:
The school of hard Knocks, Il

Dates:
15 to 20 years   —   N/A

Location:
Global Territories

Degree/Level Attained:
Supervising Dealer and Associate

Description:

Maintained a position less likely to be filled by woman Dealer/Associate among hard hitting thugs and big time Dealers from the East Coast with a minimal amount of time served. While missing out on the real joys of having a life. Avoided being killed through the grace and mercy of God in order to fulfill destiny that he had already planned out for my life. Learned the ins and outs of the dope game, moving from one level of damnation to the next. From my mistakes I grew more aware of the intent of the possibilities of my own death. Changed the recourse of my innate future by turning my power and my will over to a loving and caring God as I understand him. Made the necessary steps to improve my life and that of those around me.

Accomplishments:

- Studied the habits of drug users and dealers for about 10-15 years.

- Gained Associations by being at the wrong place at the wrong time.

- Used my personality in trouble shooting areas to gain entry in forbidden zones.

- Created a negative lifestyle along with negative associates that I can not use as a reference

- Spent all of my time degrading not only myself but those that I came in contact with

- Lived by example by showing others the wrong way to live or possibly die

- Know living to make known that the wages of sin is death But the gift of God is eternal life

Affiliations

Organization:
Unavailable

Dates:
The past   —   N/A

Affiliation/Role:
To Teach & Provide necessary
Tools of my own survival

Skills

Description:

The command of God's works over my life. Gift of Gab, Customer Service Friendly (except in troubleshooting areas where prayer is then required), Charm, Charisma and an Educational based Foundation stemming from the fountain of life. The ability to now think before acting on feelings and emotions. The ability to fit in positions otherwise thought to be unreasonable i.e. a thief would make a great head of security, a hustler would make a great sales associate, a drug manufacture would make a great pharmacist, a drug addict would make great counselor/advertisement/ whatever because of past experience's would be able to fill many positions because their interpersonal skills of appealing to what ever situation he or she found herself in.

Interests

Description:

Making amends by...
Enlightening the world with my story, with a confirmation that this resume will allow you to see; where people of my sort can best fit in a world that has discriminated against for far too long.

You say people can change or at least you think they can, all that I am asking is for a chance with out making the road more then a natural to spiritual battle field.

Assist us by allowing us a real chance to redeem ourselves (with out all of the red tape/politics). Assist us by reevaluating the terms for which you have viewed us spoiled and inefficient. Some of us had no real knowledge of the amount of soulful pain our decisions would lead us to and we have grown from our mistakes and have paid for our crimes. How long must we continue to pay? These convictions though they may not be life sentences behind bars we are still being held accountable as if we were.

Summary:

I implore you to review my criminal background and look at what you see standing or sitting before you and make your decision based on the strength you see and the God given knowledge you hold within yourself. Some of my references are unavailable due to them being dead, locked up or their where about's unknown. After viewing my resume then and only then will you know where I would best benefit you in your business adventures and I look forward to being the best at what you determine to suit me with. I also maintain the possibilities for advancement within your company.

Thank you for your time.

Professional References

Name:	**Company:**
John F. Hannah	New Life Covenant Oakwood Church

Telephone Number:	**Job Title:**
Upon Request	Pastor

Name:	**Company:**
L. Fox	Criminal Court for the city of Chicago

Telephone Number:	**Job Title:**
Upon request	Judge

Let's Suppose…

Let's just suppose I had been terribly depressed so depressed that I became a crack head/ dope fiend and I sold drugs to further my drug usage and ruined lives in the midst of it all, and not necessarily in that order…

Lets just suppose I went to prison did time got out and couldn't find a job and became even more depressed that my only objective was to get high until I died thus saving everyone around me heart ache and drama (so I thought). While we're at it, let's suppose that my depression started early on in life.

I was the eldest daughter of three which turned out to be four by way of my father who by the way was not really my father had another child right after he fathered my brother let's suppose.

Let's suppose then, that not long after that a sister was born to my mother, thus turning us into three siblings by my mother and let's not forget; one by another woman with the gentleman that's really not my father which incidentally I found out about at the tender age of ten years old.

Ok, ok I know that this is a lot of supposing but let's go see and do… lets just suppose.

Please let us continue,

Now; as a child let's suppose that I was molested by the church organist and my cousin. Let's also suppose that I grew up in one of those churches that had strict rules and harsh regulations and I didn't get to really live out my childhood because of these rules. I couldn't take gym or any activities because boys would be there and I wasn't allowed to wear shorts again because boys would be there oh and because Deuteronomy 5:22 says that women shouldn't wear pants. So then all that was left for me to get to know and play with were girls. Let's also say that I witnessed my father who wasn't my biological father beat my mother inches into death.

I got pregnant at seventeen, and then my first lover was a woman oh and I was put out at 12:00 for being late for curfew later raped that night and then moved to Harvey where I engaged in a relationship with my step brother from the marriage after my adopted father (whom I call Daddy). Let's also suppose that I became wild & crazy and looked forward to drinking and dancing until men fought over me or the club closed (buck wild). Let's just say that although I found that men frightened me I found them to be marks and I decided to be with women because they were more affectionate and seemed to never pose a threat physically. (Wrong)

I was told that I'd burn in hell forever and so I tried to be with men for the sake of saving my hide which in turn lead me down the roads of having more children without present father's and becoming more depressed because I hadn't taken the time to really get to know myself because I had been to busy trying to escape. Escape life as I had known it to be with out ever figuring out that I could change things so I spiraled to even deeper depths of ruin.

I immersed myself in parties, drugs and lesbian relationships, I tried to go to school but then there was my mother being busy behind me plotting to take my children to enlarge her pockets, so I turned to drugs again to numb the pain… Now, now…we are just supposing. Don't get yourself all up in an uproar! (Or do)

OK…

She has three of my children by way of calling the alphabet people on me and raging on about my lesbian affairs and how awful my lovers were to me. Truth be told…in any relationship there are problems and nosy (or concerned) mothers. My guess is that when she found out that there was money in raising some one else's children she jumped at the chance.

Well! I 'm not going to suppose all over her so let me interject here, let's say that I was making a few bad choices I hadn't learned how to have a relationship with a man. Remember I wasn't allowed to play with boys as a child and My biological father I never knew, the father that raised me and gave me his last name is my father and I saw him beat my mother remember?

You must be saying by now; did you get any counseling? Yeah, as a child my mother took me to counseling but then how does a child go into a stranger's office and tell all when growing up as a child you're taught not to talk about what goes on at home? How?

(Answers taken here)

So there I was, this broken child with all of this weight and no where to direct my questions or anger and frustrations what happens next? This same child grows up to ignore reality and run from her problems and self medicate. I suppose.

What do you suppose?

Then a fourth child is born, with everything else that has seemingly gone wrong I make a adamant decision to put all of my love into this child because the others were seemingly lost to me. I decide to turn my life around, I go to my sister have a heart to heart so to speak, I ask her to watch my daughter for one month, she agrees. While I'm gone…my mother decides that she has to interfere, she takes my fourth child applies it to the state that I'm unfit when in fact I was working, off of drugs although living in a shelter and about to move into my apartment within days. Takes my child, just takes her and gives me some plaid excuse about doctor's questions and what if's. We are still supposing here mind you. Which means either my sister didn't really want to be bothered (believable) because she had her own child to care for (understandable) so why didn't she just say so?

Why is miscommunication possible, why can't people say what they mean and mean what they say?

Meanwhile back at the ranch a sister is falling apart…again still hadn't found the necessary tools to cope with life on life's terms (sad). Time passes by with limited visitations with her children and constant drugs that were thought to ease the past pains of life without ever really getting butt naked honest with horrible repercussions. Which were usually followed by more drugs, feelings of hopelessness, failure and deep depression explosively present?

Life seemed meaningless and death seemed to be the only answer...

What do you suppose happened?

    A) did she get her life together
    B) did she over dose off of street drugs
    C) Did she commit suicide
    D) did she ever get her kids back
    E) did her and her mother reconcile
    F) did she find God
    G) has she found peace within herself
    H) Is there any hope for her
    I) how and who does this affect socially and mentally
    J) what do you think could have been done differently
    K) how can you check yourself...your family... your life

Thank you for your time of supposition.

LMJ.

LaVergne, TN USA
09 February 2011
215765LV00002B/1/P